EMMANUEL JOSEPH

The Philosophy of Progress, How Emotional Intelligence and Cultural Dynamics Drive Ethical Innovation

Copyright © 2025 by Emmanuel Joseph

All rights reserved. No part of this publication may be reproduced, stored or transmitted in any form or by any means, electronic, mechanical, photocopying, recording, scanning, or otherwise without written permission from the publisher. It is illegal to copy this book, post it to a website, or distribute it by any other means without permission.

First edition

*This book was professionally typeset on Reedsy.
Find out more at reedsy.com*

Contents

1	Chapter 1: The Genesis of Progress	1
2	Chapter 2: Emotional Intelligence – The Human Core	3
3	Chapter 3: The Fabric of Culture	5
4	Chapter 4: The Fusion of Intelligence and Culture	7
5	Chapter 5: Ethical Innovation in Business	9
6	Chapter 6: The Role of Education	11
7	Chapter 7: Public Policy and Ethical Progress	13
8	Chapter 8: Technology and Ethical Innovation	15
9	Chapter 9: The Role of Media	17
10	Chapter 10: Community Engagement and Ethical Progress	19
11	Chapter 11: Leadership and Ethical Progress	21
12	Chapter 12: The Global Perspective	23
13	Chapter 13: The Future of Work	25
14	Chapter 14: Personal Development and Ethical Progress	27
15	Chapter 15: Measuring Ethical Progress	29
16	Chapter 16: Challenges and Opportunities	31
17	Chapter 17: A Vision for the Future	33

1

Chapter 1: The Genesis of Progress

In the ever-evolving landscape of human civilization, the concept of progress remains a paramount force driving societies forward. Progress, in its essence, refers to the continuous advancement of human potential, knowledge, and capabilities. In a modern context, it encompasses technological breakthroughs, social reforms, and economic growth. At the core of this evolution are two powerful elements: emotional intelligence and cultural dynamics. These elements not only shape the trajectory of progress but also influence how ethical innovation is perceived and implemented.

A glance through history reveals varied interpretations of progress. Ancient civilizations like the Greeks and Romans pursued progress through philosophical inquiry and engineering marvels, while the Renaissance period marked a rebirth of art and science. The Industrial Revolution propelled societies into an era of unprecedented technological advancements, transforming everyday life. Each epoch's definition of progress was shaped by its unique cultural context and prevailing values, underscoring the intricate relationship between societal norms and advancement.

In contemporary society, the notion of ethical innovation has gained prominence, emphasizing the need for advancements that are not only groundbreaking but also morally sound. Ethical innovation is the practice of integrating ethical considerations into the process of creating new technologies, policies, and practices. This approach ensures that innovations contribute positively to society, mitigate harm, and respect human rights. The importance of ethical innovation cannot be overstated, as it fosters trust, sustainability, and social responsibility.

The intersection of emotional intelligence and cultural dynamics plays a pivotal role in fostering ethical innovation. Emotional intelligence, defined as the ability to recognize, understand, and manage one's emotions, enhances interpersonal relationships and decision-making processes. Cultural dynamics, on the other hand, encompass the shared values, beliefs, and practices that shape a society. Together, these elements create a framework for ethical innovation, guiding individuals and organizations towards choices that reflect both emotional acumen and cultural sensitivity.

2

Chapter 2: Emotional Intelligence – The Human Core

Emotional intelligence (EI) is a vital aspect of human interaction, defined as the ability to recognize, understand, and manage our emotions and those of others. Daniel Goleman, a pioneer in this field, outlined five key components of EI: self-awareness, self-regulation, motivation, empathy, and social skills. These components form the foundation of effective communication, collaboration, and leadership, allowing individuals to navigate complex social environments with ease.

The impact of emotional intelligence on personal and professional relationships cannot be overstated. In personal settings, EI fosters deeper connections, trust, and mutual respect. It enables individuals to navigate conflicts gracefully and maintain healthy relationships. In professional environments, EI enhances teamwork, fosters a positive work culture, and drives productivity. Leaders with high EI are better equipped to inspire and motivate their teams, leading to higher job satisfaction and overall success.

There are numerous real-world examples of leaders who embody emotional intelligence. Figures like Nelson Mandela, whose empathetic approach helped to reconcile a divided nation, and Satya Nadella, who transformed Microsoft's corporate culture by promoting empathy and collaboration, serve as shining examples. These leaders demonstrate how emotional intelligence can drive not only individual success but also organizational and societal progress.

Emotional intelligence plays a crucial role in ethical decision-making. By understanding and managing their emotions, individuals can make decisions that align with their values and principles. Empathy, a core component of EI, allows individuals to consider the perspectives and needs of others, leading to more compassionate and ethical choices. In an increasingly complex world, emotional intelligence provides a moral compass that guides individuals and organizations towards ethical innovation.

3

Chapter 3: The Fabric of Culture

Cultural dynamics refer to the patterns of behavior, beliefs, and values that characterize a society. These dynamics influence how individuals perceive the world, interact with others, and make decisions. In today's globalized world, understanding cultural dynamics is more important than ever, as it allows for effective communication and collaboration across diverse cultural contexts.

Cultural contexts play a significant role in shaping behaviors, values, and ethics. For example, collectivist cultures, such as those in East Asia, prioritize group harmony and consensus, while individualist cultures, like those in the United States, emphasize personal autonomy and self-expression. These cultural differences impact how individuals approach problem-solving, conflict resolution, and innovation, highlighting the importance of cultural awareness in driving progress.

Cultural diversity is a powerful catalyst for innovation. Diverse teams bring unique perspectives, ideas, and approaches to problem-solving, leading to more creative and effective solutions. Companies like Google and IBM have harnessed the power of cultural diversity to drive innovation and maintain a competitive edge. By fostering an inclusive environment, these organizations have unlocked the full potential of their diverse workforce.

To illustrate the impact of cultural diversity on innovation, consider the case of Unilever. This multinational corporation has embraced cultural diversity by creating diverse teams and promoting inclusive practices. As a result, Unilever has developed innovative products that cater to the needs of a global market, driving both social and economic progress. The company's success demonstrates the value of cultural diversity in fostering ethical innovation.

4

Chapter 4: The Fusion of Intelligence and Culture

The interaction between emotional intelligence and cultural dynamics creates a powerful synergy that drives ethical innovation. Emotional intelligence enables individuals to navigate complex social environments, while cultural dynamics provide the context in which these interactions occur. Together, these elements create a holistic approach to progress that considers both individual and collective well-being.

Cultural empathy is a crucial aspect of emotionally intelligent leadership. By understanding and appreciating the cultural backgrounds of their team members, leaders can foster an inclusive and supportive environment. This cultural empathy enhances communication, collaboration, and trust, leading to more effective and ethical decision-making. Leaders who demonstrate cultural empathy are better equipped to navigate the complexities of a globalized world.

Cultural understanding also enhances emotional intelligence. Exposure to diverse cultural contexts broadens individuals' perspectives, allowing them to develop greater empathy and social skills. For example, individuals who have lived and worked in different countries often demonstrate higher levels of emotional intelligence, as they have learned to navigate and adapt to various cultural norms and expectations. This cultural understanding enriches their emotional intelligence and fosters ethical innovation.

To develop both emotional and cultural intelligence, leaders can adopt various strategies. These include promoting diversity and inclusion initiatives, providing cultural competence training, and encouraging open dialogue about cultural differences. By creating an environment that values and respects cultural diversity, organizations can enhance emotional intelligence, drive ethical innovation, and achieve sustainable progress.

5

Chapter 5: Ethical Innovation in Business

Ethical innovation in business involves creating new products, services, and processes that are not only effective but also morally sound. This approach prioritizes the well-being of all stakeholders, including employees, customers, and the broader community. Ethical innovation ensures that businesses contribute positively to society while maintaining their competitive edge.

Maintaining ethics in innovation can be challenging, as it often involves balancing competing interests and navigating complex moral dilemmas. For example, businesses may face pressure to prioritize short-term profits over long-term sustainability or to compromise on ethical standards to stay ahead of competitors. However, by integrating ethical considerations into their innovation processes, businesses can build trust, foster loyalty, and achieve long-term success.

Several companies have successfully integrated ethics into their innovation processes. Patagonia, a leading outdoor apparel company, is renowned for its commitment to environmental sustainability and ethical business practices. By prioritizing sustainable materials and fair labor practices, Patagonia has set a high standard for ethical innovation in the industry. Similarly, Ben & Jerry's, an ice cream company, has consistently championed social justice causes, demonstrating that businesses can drive positive change while remaining profitable.

To foster ethical innovation, organizations can adopt various practical steps. These include establishing clear ethical guidelines, promoting a culture of transparency and accountability, and encouraging employee engagement in ethical decision-making. By embedding ethics into their innovation processes, businesses can create products and services that not only meet market demands but also contribute to a better world.

6

Chapter 6: The Role of Education

Education plays a pivotal role in developing emotional intelligence and cultural awareness. From early childhood to higher education, educational institutions have the responsibility to nurture these skills. By integrating emotional intelligence and cultural dynamics into curricula, educators can prepare students to navigate the complexities of a diverse and interconnected world, fostering ethical innovation.

There are numerous educational programs that emphasize emotional intelligence and cultural awareness. For example, social-emotional learning (SEL) programs in schools focus on developing students' self-awareness, self-management, social awareness, relationship skills, and responsible decision-making. These programs equip students with the tools they need to succeed in both personal and professional settings, promoting ethical behavior and innovation.

Educators play a crucial role in fostering ethical innovation. By modeling emotional intelligence and cultural competence, teachers can create a positive and inclusive classroom environment. Additionally, educators can design lessons and activities that encourage students to think critically about ethical dilemmas and consider diverse perspectives. By promoting ethical thinking and behavior, educators can inspire the next generation of ethical innovators.

To integrate emotional and cultural intelligence into curricula, schools can adopt various strategies. These include incorporating SEL programs, promoting multicultural education, and encouraging project-based learning that addresses real-world ethical challenges. By providing students with opportunities to develop these skills, educational institutions can contribute to a more ethical and innovative society.

7

Chapter 7: Public Policy and Ethical Progress

Government policies play a significant role in promoting ethical innovation. By creating a regulatory framework that encourages ethical behavior, governments can ensure that businesses and individuals prioritize the well-being of society. Policies that support emotional intelligence and cultural dynamics can further enhance ethical innovation, fostering a more inclusive and sustainable future.

Several policies support emotional intelligence and cultural dynamics. For example, public health policies that promote mental well-being and social cohesion can enhance emotional intelligence at the societal level. Similarly, policies that encourage cultural diversity and inclusion, such as anti-discrimination laws and multicultural education initiatives, can foster cultural awareness and empathy, driving ethical progress.

There are successful public policies in different countries that promote ethical innovation. In Sweden, for example, the government has implemented policies that support social innovation and sustainability. These policies have created a conducive environment for ethical businesses to thrive, contributing to the country's overall progress. Similarly, in Japan, policies that promote work-life balance and mental health have enhanced emotional intelligence in the workplace, driving ethical innovation.

To further promote ethical innovation, governments can adopt various recommendations. These include creating incentives for businesses to prioritize ethical practices, investing in education and training programs that develop emotional and cultural intelligence, and fostering collaboration between public and private sectors. By implementing these strategies, governments can create a supportive environment for ethical progress.

8

Chapter 8: Technology and Ethical Innovation

The relationship between technology and ethical innovation is complex and multifaceted. On one hand, technology has the potential to drive significant progress, creating new opportunities and solving pressing global challenges. On the other hand, technological advancements often raise ethical concerns, such as privacy, security, and the potential for misuse. Balancing these considerations is crucial for ensuring that technology serves the greater good.

Emerging technologies, such as artificial intelligence (AI), blockchain, and biotechnology, have significant ethical implications. For example, AI has the potential to revolutionize industries and improve quality of life, but it also raises concerns about bias, job displacement, and privacy. Similarly, biotechnology offers promising solutions for healthcare and agriculture but poses ethical questions related to genetic modification and access to resources. Addressing these concerns requires a thoughtful and inclusive approach to innovation.

Several tech companies are leading the way in ethical innovation. For example, Microsoft has committed to developing AI technologies that prioritize fairness, accountability, and transparency. The company has established ethical guidelines and created a dedicated AI Ethics Board to ensure that its technologies align with these principles. Similarly, IBM has implemented policies to address bias in AI and promote ethical data usage, demonstrating a commitment to ethical innovation.

To create ethically sound technology solutions, organizations can adopt various guidelines. These include establishing clear ethical principles, conducting thorough impact assessments, involving diverse stakeholders in the innovation process, and promoting transparency and accountability. By integrating these practices into their technology development processes, organizations can ensure that their innovations contribute positively to society.

9

Chapter 9: The Role of Media

Media plays a crucial role in shaping emotional intelligence and cultural dynamics. As a powerful tool for communication and information dissemination, media influences how individuals perceive and understand the world around them. By promoting positive narratives and ethical values, media organizations can contribute to the development of emotional intelligence and cultural awareness, driving ethical innovation.

Media organizations have ethical responsibilities to ensure that their content promotes accurate, fair, and inclusive representation. This includes avoiding sensationalism, bias, and harmful stereotypes, and instead focusing on stories that highlight diverse perspectives and promote empathy and understanding. By adhering to these ethical standards, media organizations can foster a more informed and compassionate society.

There are several media campaigns that have successfully promoted ethical innovation. For example, the #HeForShe campaign by UN Women leveraged media to raise awareness about gender equality and encourage men to support women's rights. This campaign not only promoted cultural awareness but also inspired positive social change. Similarly, the "Like a Girl" campaign by Always challenged gender stereotypes and empowered young girls, demonstrating the power of media to drive ethical progress.

To support ethical progress, media organizations can adopt various strategies. These include promoting diverse voices and perspectives, creating content that fosters empathy and understanding, and collaborating with organizations that promote ethical innovation. By leveraging their influence, media organizations can contribute to a more ethical and inclusive society.

10

Chapter 10: Community Engagement and Ethical Progress

Community involvement is a cornerstone of ethical innovation. When communities actively participate in the development and implementation of new ideas, the resulting innovations are more likely to address local needs and reflect shared values. Engaging with communities fosters a sense of ownership and accountability, ensuring that progress benefits everyone.

Communities can play a vital role in fostering emotional intelligence and cultural awareness. By promoting inclusivity and encouraging open dialogue, communities can create environments where individuals feel valued and understood. Community-led initiatives, such as cultural festivals, support groups, and educational workshops, can enhance emotional and cultural intelligence, driving ethical progress.

There are numerous examples of community-led ethical innovation initiatives. For instance, in the town of Totnes in the UK, the Transition Towns movement has empowered residents to develop sustainable solutions to environmental challenges. By harnessing local knowledge and resources, the community has implemented projects that promote renewable energy, local food production, and waste reduction. This grassroots approach demonstrates the power of community engagement in driving ethical progress.

To engage communities in ethical progress, practical steps can be taken. These include fostering partnerships between local organizations, providing platforms for community voices to be heard, and supporting grassroots initiatives. By empowering communities to take an active role in innovation, we can ensure that progress is inclusive, equitable, and sustainable.

11

Chapter 11: Leadership and Ethical Progress

Ethical progress requires leaders who possess a unique combination of qualities, including integrity, empathy, and vision. These leaders prioritize the well-being of their stakeholders and make decisions that align with their values and principles. By embodying these qualities, ethical leaders inspire others to follow their example and drive positive change.

Emotional intelligence is a crucial component of effective leadership. Leaders who demonstrate high levels of emotional intelligence are better equipped to understand and manage their own emotions, as well as those of their team members. This emotional acumen enhances communication, fosters trust, and promotes collaboration, creating a positive and productive work environment.

Cultural awareness is equally important in leadership. By understanding and appreciating the diverse cultural backgrounds of their team members, leaders can create an inclusive environment that values and respects differences. This cultural competence enhances decision-making, as leaders are able to consider diverse perspectives and develop solutions that reflect the needs of all stakeholders.

There are numerous examples of leaders who have successfully driven ethical innovation. For instance, Paul Polman, former CEO of Unilever, championed sustainability and social responsibility, transforming the company's approach to business. Under his leadership, Unilever implemented initiatives to reduce its environmental footprint and improve the well-being of its employees and communities. Polman's commitment to ethical leadership serves as an inspiration for others to follow.

12

Chapter 12: The Global Perspective

In an increasingly interconnected world, a global perspective is essential for ethical innovation. By considering the diverse needs and values of people around the world, we can develop solutions that address global challenges and promote inclusive progress. This global mindset fosters collaboration, empathy, and mutual understanding, driving ethical innovation on a broader scale.

Different cultures approach progress and innovation in unique ways. For example, in Scandinavian countries, a strong emphasis on social welfare and environmental sustainability has led to innovative policies and practices that promote well-being and equity. In contrast, many Asian countries prioritize rapid technological advancement and economic growth, driving innovation through investment in research and development. Understanding these diverse approaches allows us to learn from each other and develop more holistic solutions.

There are numerous case studies of global initiatives that promote ethical innovation. For instance, the United Nations Sustainable Development Goals (SDGs) provide a framework for addressing global challenges such as poverty, inequality, and climate change. By fostering international collaboration and encouraging countries to adopt sustainable practices, the SDGs have inspired numerous innovative projects and policies that contribute to ethical progress.

To foster global collaboration on ethical progress, various strategies can be adopted. These include promoting cross-cultural exchange programs, supporting international research partnerships, and encouraging multinational organizations to adopt ethical standards. By embracing a global perspective, we can develop solutions that reflect the diverse needs of humanity and drive ethical innovation on a global scale.

13

Chapter 13: The Future of Work

The future workplace will be shaped by emotional intelligence and cultural dynamics. As technology continues to transform industries, the demand for soft skills, such as empathy, communication, and cultural competence, will increase. These skills are essential for navigating the complexities of a diverse and rapidly changing work environment.

Technology will play a significant role in the evolving work environment. Automation, artificial intelligence, and remote work will become more prevalent, creating new opportunities and challenges. While technology can enhance productivity and innovation, it also raises ethical concerns related to job displacement, privacy, and the potential for bias. Addressing these concerns requires a thoughtful and inclusive approach to technological development.

Ethics will be a central consideration in future work practices. As organizations strive to balance profitability with social responsibility, ethical decision-making will become increasingly important. Companies that prioritize ethical practices will build trust with their stakeholders, foster loyalty, and achieve long-term success. This ethical focus will also drive innovation, as businesses develop solutions that address societal challenges and promote sustainability.

To prepare for the future of work, organizations can adopt various recommendations. These include investing in employee development programs that enhance emotional intelligence and cultural competence, promoting ethical standards in technology development, and fostering a culture of transparency and accountability. By embracing these strategies, organizations can navigate the challenges of the future workplace and drive ethical innovation.

14

Chapter 14: Personal Development and Ethical Progress

Personal development is essential for fostering ethical progress. By continually striving to improve our emotional intelligence and cultural awareness, we can make more informed and compassionate decisions. Personal growth not only enhances our individual well-being but also contributes to the collective progress of society.

There are various strategies for developing emotional intelligence and cultural awareness. These include self-reflection, mindfulness practices, and seeking out diverse experiences. By engaging in activities that promote self-awareness and empathy, we can enhance our emotional intelligence. Similarly, by exposing ourselves to different cultures through travel, literature, and conversations, we can develop a deeper understanding of cultural dynamics.

There are numerous examples of individuals who have driven ethical innovation through personal growth. For instance, Mahatma Gandhi's commitment to nonviolent resistance and social justice was deeply rooted in his personal development journey. By cultivating empathy and cultural awareness, Gandhi was able to inspire positive change and drive ethical progress. His example demonstrates the power of personal growth in shaping ethical innovation.

To support personal development in ethical progress, practical steps can be taken. These include setting personal goals for emotional and cultural growth, seeking out mentors and role models, and engaging in continuous learning. By prioritizing our personal development, we can contribute to a more ethical and innovative society.

15

Chapter 15: Measuring Ethical Progress

Measuring ethical progress is crucial for ensuring that our efforts are effective and aligned with our values. By establishing clear metrics and indicators, we can track our progress and identify areas for improvement. This measurement process provides accountability and helps us stay focused on our ethical goals.

There are various metrics and indicators of ethical innovation. These include social impact assessments, sustainability metrics, and ethical audits. By evaluating the social, environmental, and economic impacts of our innovations, we can ensure that they contribute positively to society. Ethical audits, which assess an organization's adherence to ethical standards, provide valuable insights into areas for improvement.

Several organizations have successfully measured ethical progress. For example, B Lab, a nonprofit organization, assesses companies' social and environmental performance through the B Impact Assessment. This assessment evaluates various aspects of a company's operations, including governance, community impact, and environmental practices. By providing a comprehensive measure of ethical performance, B Lab enables companies to track their progress and make informed decisions.

To develop effective measurement tools for ethical progress, various recommendations can be adopted. These include involving diverse stakeholders in the measurement process, establishing clear and transparent criteria, and regularly reviewing and updating metrics. By creating robust and inclusive measurement frameworks, we can ensure that our efforts to drive ethical innovation are effective and aligned with our values.

16

Chapter 16: Challenges and Opportunities

Promoting ethical innovation comes with its own set of challenges. These include balancing competing interests, navigating complex moral dilemmas, and addressing resistance to change. Additionally, there may be structural barriers, such as regulatory constraints or limited resources, that hinder ethical progress.

Despite these challenges, there are numerous opportunities for driving ethical innovation. For example, advances in technology offer new possibilities for creating sustainable solutions and addressing global challenges. Similarly, growing awareness of social and environmental issues provides a platform for promoting ethical practices and inspiring positive change.

There are several case studies of organizations that have overcome challenges to drive ethical progress. For instance, Interface, a leading manufacturer of modular carpets, faced significant environmental challenges due to the nature of its industry. However, the company embraced sustainability as a core value and implemented innovative practices, such as using recycled materials and reducing waste. As a result, Interface has become a pioneer in sustainable business practices, demonstrating that ethical innovation is possible even in challenging industries.

To address challenges and seize opportunities, various strategies can be adopted. These include fostering a culture of innovation and collaboration, investing in research and development, and engaging with diverse stakeholders.

By embracing these strategies, organizations can navigate the complexities of ethical innovation and drive positive change.

17

Chapter 17: A Vision for the Future

The journey through this book has explored the intricate relationship between emotional intelligence, cultural dynamics, and ethical innovation. These elements are interconnected and collectively contribute to the progress of society. By understanding and harnessing their power, we can drive meaningful and sustainable change.

Ongoing commitment to ethical innovation is essential for creating a better future. This commitment requires continuous reflection, learning, and adaptation. By prioritizing ethical considerations in our decisions and actions, we can build a more just, inclusive, and sustainable world.

A vision for the future of progress is one where emotional intelligence and cultural dynamics are at the forefront of innovation. In this future, organizations and individuals alike embrace empathy, diversity, and ethical principles. This approach not only fosters innovation but also ensures that progress benefits everyone, creating a more equitable and harmonious society.

As we conclude this journey, let us embrace the call to action for engaging in ethical progress. Whether in our personal lives, professional endeavors, or community involvement, we all have the power to drive positive change. By cultivating emotional intelligence and cultural awareness, we can contribute to a future where ethical innovation thrives and progress is truly inclusive.

The Philosophy of Progress: How Emotional Intelligence and Cultural Dynamics Drive Ethical Innovation

In today's rapidly evolving world, the pursuit of progress is more than a quest for technological advancements—it's an intricate dance between emotional intelligence, cultural dynamics, and ethical innovation. "The Philosophy of Progress" delves into this fascinating intersection, uncovering how our emotions and cultural contexts shape the innovations that drive our society forward.

From historical milestones to contemporary breakthroughs, this book offers a profound exploration of how emotional intelligence enhances interpersonal relationships, fosters ethical decision-making, and empowers leaders to inspire positive change. By examining the rich tapestry of cultural dynamics, readers will gain insights into how diverse perspectives and values contribute to creative and sustainable solutions.

Each chapter weaves together theory and real-world examples, presenting a comprehensive framework for understanding and implementing ethical innovation. Discover the transformative power of community engagement, the pivotal role of education, and the influence of public policy in promoting a more inclusive and responsible future.

Whether you're a leader, educator, policymaker, or simply a curious mind, "The Philosophy of Progress" provides the tools and inspiration needed to navigate the complexities of our modern world. Embrace the call to action and join the movement towards a brighter, more equitable future where emotional intelligence and cultural awareness pave the way for ethical innovation.

www.ingramcontent.com/pod-product-compliance
Lightning Source LLC
LaVergne TN
LVHW020739090526
838202LV00057BA/6045